HOW TO SPOT AND DEAL WITH
HATERS

E. J. TYLER

Copyright © 2013 E. J. Tyler.

All rights reserved. No part of this book may be reproduced, stored, or transmitted by any means—whether auditory, graphic, mechanical, or electronic—without written permission of both publisher and author, except in the case of brief excerpts used in critical articles and reviews. Unauthorized reproduction of any part of this work is illegal and is punishable by law.

ISBN: 978-1-4834-0570-4 (sc)
ISBN: 978-1-4834-0572-8 (hc)
ISBN: 978-1-4834-0571-1 (e)

Library of Congress Control Number: 2013921978

Because of the dynamic nature of the Internet, any web addresses or links contained in this book may have changed since publication and may no longer be valid. The views expressed in this work are solely those of the author and do not necessarily reflect the views of the publisher, and the publisher hereby disclaims any responsibility for them.

Any people depicted in stock imagery provided by Thinkstock are models, and such images are being used for illustrative purposes only. Certain stock imagery © Thinkstock.

Lulu Publishing Services rev. date: 12/10/2013

This book is dedicated to my son Eric (EJ) Tyler Jr. Not a day goes by when I don't think of you. You taught me so much in the little but valuable time you were here. One lesson that stands out among all is that no one is promised tomorrow, so live life every day to its fullest. I now have the strength and determination to do things that might not have been possible for me, and for that, I say thanks. All I ask is that you help me protect and watch over your sisters, because you know you were always their big brother. Man, this is hard. Rest in peace, EJ. Oh yeah, I took your name (EJ); hope you don't mind. See ya later, son.

My Louisiana saint, 12/14/2009–04/28/2012

Love, Dad

CONTENTS

Introduction ix

1 Why This Book Was Needed ix
2 Friends Who Hate 1
    How Can I Tell If My Friends Are Hating? 5
    But I Like Hanging with This Person, and We
    Have the Same Friends 7
    I Know He or She Is Hating, but the Person Can't
    Hurt Me 8
    Money and Friends 8
    Conclusion 10
3 Don't Give Haters Any Power 11
    The Instigator 14
    Every Time the Hater Sees My Friends, He or
    She Has Something to Say about Me 15
    Conclusion 16

4   Can My Kinfolk Be Hating? 19
      Rich Family Members Who Hate 22
      Ghetto-Fabulous Family Members Who Hate 23
      Conclusion 24

5   Haters on the Job 25
      What If It's My Boss Who's Hating? 29
      Conclusion 30

6   Not My Siblings Too! 31
      Man, I Think My Momma's Hating 34
      Man, I Think My Daddy's Hating 34
      Conclusion 35

7   Man, I Think I'm the Hater 37
      The Two Types of Haters 39
      Man, I Know I'm Hating 41
      Conclusion 42

8   Don't Even Know Me and Hate Me 43
      Haters Are Like the Flu—They're Contagious 46
      I Trust My Source 48
      Conclusion 48

9   Man, Not in the Church! 51
      She Didn't Have to Dress Like That 53
      He or She Always Has to Sing 55
      Why Do They Put So Much in Church? 56
      I Hate the Way He or She Preaches 57
      Conclusion 58

Summary 59

About the Author 69

INTRODUCTION
WHY THIS BOOK WAS NEEDED

For the last couple of years, I have heard the term *haters* everywhere, used to describe a person who simply is jealous or envious of another person. I never gave it much thought, because I knew what a hater was, but when I heard a famous preacher on TV using the terminology, I knew it was big. I thought to myself, if this preacher took the time to preach a whole sermon on haters, it had to be a problem, not only out in the world but also in his church.

If you are reading this book, you are probably curious about why these haters do what they do. Let me explain. Have you ever been criticized for absolutely nothing? Have you ever been lied on and didn't know why? Have you ever been talked about for no reason at all (or so you thought)? If so, then this book is for you.

In this book, not only do I explain why haters hate, but I also show you who's doing the hating and how to handle them. The aim of this book is to make you aware of people who might not have your best interest in mind so you will know how to acknowledge the threat and how to handle it.

Most people are surrounded by haters every day, and the bad thing is, we don't even know it, and that can be dangerous.

The only time most of you will figure out these people are hating on you is when you start doing positive things, and by then, sometimes it's too late. The reason I say that is because if this person is a close friend of yours, believe me, in some form or fashion, he or she has been purposely stopping you from moving forward. You just couldn't see the signs, because maybe you didn't think a friend would do something like that—wish that you don't succeed. That is one of the reasons I've written this book: to give people a heads-up on all the signs and tricks these people use.

You might ask, "Well, EJ, what makes you an expert on this subject?" My answer is, "Life and the experience it brings." I was once surrounded by haters and didn't even know it until I got involved with a network-marketing company. That company opened my eyes to another world of positive thinking and positive people who produce positive results. For that positive change, I have to thank a man named Ron (a.k.a. "Chief"). He warned me about all the problematic haters I would have to endure for this positive change.

When he invited me to sit with him up front at a national convention one year, he made me realize how much more life had to offer. The energy up there was very intense; everyone was smiling and highly motivated. I could literally feel the positive energy. From that day forward, I was transformed. I never wanted to sit in the back of a room again, no matter where I was, because I knew the energy was up front.

While we were sitting there, he leaned over and said something to me that I'll never forget: "I can either see you *at* the top or *from* the top. It's your choice, but whatever you do, don't quit." He also had another saying that went like this: "Network marketing may not be what you want to do for the rest of your life, but it can be the vehicle that takes you to where you want to go." How true.

Be cool, Chief, and thanks for everything. You put me on the path, and I truly recommend that company because of its leadership, training, and objective to put people first.

How to spot and deal with haters is going to make you think. It is also going to wake you up to the reality of the world—that some people mean you no good and want you to stay right where you are. There is nothing you can do about it, as far as changing their way of thinking. So get ready for the ride of your life.

Oh, by the way, some of you may be sleeping with the enemy.

CHAPTER 1

FRIENDS WHO HATE

All my life, I've heard warnings such as, "Watch who you hang with"; "Show me your friends, and I'll show you your future"; and "Birds of a feather flock together." There is one kind of person on earth who is the opposite of a friend, and that is a hater. Some people may want to argue that an enemy is the opposite of a friend, but I can prove that some enemies are mirror images of their adversaries. That is why, when some enemies put aside their differences and work out their problems, they become best friends. A hater, on the other hand, will *never* put aside his or her differences, because there's nothing you can do or give to him or her that will make the hater like you.

I have witnessed and been the victim of a hater, who simply is jealous of another person because of who that person is, what that person is becoming, or what that person has. The hater perceives that he or she doesn't measure up to that person.

If you don't believe me, first find a hater—which shouldn't be hard to do, because haters are everywhere—maybe even one of your friends. You know, the friend who takes a jab at everything you say or do. Yes, that person is a hater, but I am sure you already knew that, right?

Here is the kicker: If you are friendly with someone who is a hater, why is that person your friend? Why is that person invited to your house? Why do you have that person's number in your cell phone? I'll tell you why—because you tolerate that person and his or her offensive behavior. But friends should *celebrate* your successes, not *tolerate* them.

For whatever reason, you allow someone to hate on you, and it's not good. Maybe you feel obligated to be that person's friend because you grew up together, he or she doesn't have other friends (I wonder why!), or he or she is going through a tough time. The point is that haters are usually always going through hard times; most of them are bitter, always complaining about something, or always moody and finding fault in everything around them. How can a person live like that? I'm getting depressed just thinking about it, so let's move on.

You may be thinking that I'm telling you to throw away a friendship simply because someone complains a lot or is always moody. The answer is yes, end the friendship. If that person is getting moody or even hates you simply because you are doing well or "moving on up", then that person is not your friend. You can't hang out with negative people and expect to live a positive life.

I know the road to success goes right through the dump; you have to go through something to have something. But just because you went through the dump, or even if you came out of that dump, it doesn't mean you have to bring trash with you. Some people are better off staying where they want to be: in the dump.

The higher you go in life, the more things will change, like your finances, friends, and future, but not until you change.

Here's an example of why some of your so-called friends should be cut off. I once had a friend I call "Undercover Hater." We did everything together until I bought a fully loaded (though used) 1992 royal-blue Cadillac Deville.

The first person I wanted to show it to was this friend. When I finally caught up with him, I was burning with excitement and ready to ride. The first thing he said to me was, "Boy, you think you somebody now, huh?"

I blew it off as a joke and asked him if he wanted to cut some corners. He told me no; he had something to do. So I told him, "Maybe later," but later never came.

At that moment, my friend became jealous to the point that if other people complimented my car, he would say something bad about it. Eventually, he started telling people he wished something bad would happen to the car.

The more I tried to show him that we were still cool—letting him use the car and everything—the more he resented me, to the point where I could feel his jealousy. All of this was over a five-year-old used car. This guy is jealous of me to this day.

How Can I Tell If My Friends Are Hating?

There are several ways to determine whether your friends are hating, but here are some of the key things to look for.

1. Negativity: As soon as you do something or buy something, a hater will try to make it seem insignificant or unappealing, never giving compliments and trying

to get others to feel the same way by pointing out flaws.

2. Jealousy: As soon as you buy something new, a hater either has to get one too or top the one that you got. If the hater can't get it, then he or she doesn't want you to bring yours around or even talk about it. If you do bring it around or talk about it, the hater will just say that you're showing off.

3. Anger: As soon as you say something, the hater is quick to become confrontational with you, disapproving of anything you say or do. Most of the time, this ends with the two of you arguing. (Note: Never argue with a hater. He or she isn't arguing to prove a point; he or she is arguing to make you look bad by any means necessary, like revealing secrets that shouldn't be revealed.)

4. Hatred: Hatred is the most powerful feeling, especially the hatred of a person who is supposed to be your friend. You may not see the person hating on you or even hear about it, but you can just feel it sometimes by the way the person looks at you or even talks to you. (Note: Undercover hating is the worst kind because it is a friend trying to hide his or her true feelings, and if he or she can inflict any kind of harm and not be noticed, this person will do it. Get rid of this person immediately, because he or she is a snake.)

"Hate does more to the hater than it does to the hated; it hardens their heart."—Dr. Martin Luther King Jr.

But I Like Hanging with This Person, and We Have the Same Friends

This is a tricky, sensitive subject; you don't want to stop socializing with your friend because of one person. This is what you should do.

Discuss the matter with your closest friends (no more than three). God help you if you think you have ten good, loyal friends you can talk to about anything. If you think you do, stop reading this book for a second and slap yourself back to reality.

If your true friends also notice the person acting like a hater, if they see what you clearly see and feel, let your friends know that you won't be hanging with that person any longer. Believe me, your true friends will understand and, in most cases, will be on board with your decision. They may even follow suit. (Note: elephant-in-the-room syndrome is when something is obvious but no one say anything.)

Do not feel bad about the decision you've made. Don't feel that you need to give the hater another chance; believe me, you are dropping dead weight. Whether or not the person is hating on you on purpose, you're better off removing this person from your circle of influence.

The person you are walking with can determine the speed at which you walk so know who you are walking with.

I Know He or She Is Hating, but the Person Can't Hurt Me

This, my friend, is playing with fire. The person you are allowing to hang around you for your personal entertainment is biding his or her time. The moment you slip up, or the moment he or she knows anything damaging about you, he or she will use it. Guess whose fault that is? It's like playing with a snake, and when the snake bites you, you wonder how it happened—you were playing with a snake!

Have you ever heard the saying, "Keep your friends close and your enemies closer"? That's the most ridiculous thing I've ever heard. I don't want my enemy anywhere around me. My job is to contain you as much as I can, not empower you by having you close to me. Some of the most powerful men have been brought down by haters—Julius Caesar and Malcolm X, just to name a couple.

The greatest betrayer of all time came from inside the circle: Judas Iscariot. We all know how *that* story ended. Never think that a person is too small or insufficient to harm you. Arm yourself with the right information, because even an imbecile can cause havoc.

Money and Friends

The bottom line is that true friends love you regardless of what you have or don't have. They hang out with you because of who you are, not something materialistic. Friends are the people who know everything about you and still like you in spite of your shortcomings.

When it comes to money, don't let your so-called friends tell you that you've changed simply because you now have a little money. That's the reason to get money: so you can change. Here are some examples of things you *should* change:

1. **Your mind-set:** Your thinking must be the first thing you change, in order to alter your prior results. When the mind changes, results change.

2. **Your environment:** You must be aware of your surroundings. Start with your address.

3. **Your friends:** This is the most difficult thing to change, but it must be done. Only a few friends—*true friends*—will accept your positive change.

"Anytime God has blessed you, you need to look like God has done something for you." –Steve Harvey

---

Believe me, a rising tide lifts all ships, so run with whoever is on board with your positive changes. Trust me, it will benefit them too.

Another thing: stop believing that money changes the characteristics of someone's personality. If that person was an asshole before the money, he or she is probably going to be an even bigger asshole now. Money only amplifies what you already are. If you are a generous and compassionate person, then money will amplify those qualities in you.

You might be wondering, *Should I lend money to my friends?* My answer is money should never be a problem between true friends. How much money it is and what it is for should be what guides your decision. Don't get me wrong, and don't be a fool. But if you can help that person and you know he or she will truly appreciate it, then handle your business. Remember, a rising tide raises all ships.

Did you notice I didn't mention haters at all on the topic of money and friends? It's because they don't go together, like oil and water.

Conclusion

You wonder, *Are my friends hating?* The answer is yes, they probably are. You ask, *What can I do about it?* The answer is *nothing,* because the problem is not you; it's their heart. So until they change their mind-set, which will change their heart, there's nothing you can do. Why would you want to spend the time and energy trying to change people who might not want to change?

In the 1# bestseller Think & Grow Rich A Black Choice on page 49 the author quotes Booker T. Washington by saying, "The circumstances that surround a man's life are not important. How that man responds to those circumstances is important. His response is the ultimate determining factor between success and failure." So save that energy for what you'll learn in the next chapter, which is about ignoring haters completely. This is going to take a lot of energy on your part.

CHAPTER 2

DON'T GIVE HATERS ANY POWER

When I say, "Don't give these people any power," I mean *absolutely none,* because the only way haters can affect you is by what you give them. Let me clarify what I mean. For example, if a person is hating on you because you bought a new car, don't allow that person in your car. Believe me, just the fact that you haven't let him or her ride in it is killing this person. Completely ignore this person; don't spend time asking why he or she doesn't like it or what he or she finds wrong with the car.

Now let's say people are saying things about you for some reason—they don't like your hair, your car, your house, your friends, your kids, your job, your job title. I think you get the point. For whatever reason, they don't like you; this information has now gotten back to you, brought to you by the *instigator.*

I'll talk about the instigator later, but for now, you have to use him or her. When the instigator tells you what so-and-so said, don't join in that foolishness. Simply say, "I don't have time to entertain that. Besides, why should I worry about what they think about me?" You have just lit a match. Keep in mind that you didn't tell the instigator to go back and tell the people anything. But believe me, the instigator can't help him- or herself; the instigator is going to tell the haters what you said, because that's what instigators do. They keep the mess going and might even add to it, to spice it up a little.

When the instigator comes back—and he or she will, because that's what instigators do; they instigate—keep in mind that the haters are really angry with you now. It's not because you answered them back, but because of what you said ("I don't have time to entertain that. Besides, why should I worry about what they think about me?"). Remember that.

When the instigator begins to tell you what the haters said, stop him or her immediately and say, "I don't care what those people thinks. They are only hating, and I have no time for that foolishness. Please don't tell me anything about them again."

You should stop the instigator from saying what the haters said because you really don't want that foolishness in your spirit. On the contrary, you got your message through. The message? *I know you're hating on me, but I'm not going to come down to your level, because you're not important enough for me to entertain your assumption of me.*

If you are standing there, arguing with a fool, trust me— *you* are the fool. Fools hold no power, so don't give them any.

The only power a hater has is mental infliction.
If a hater is not allowed in your head, then
what he or she is doing is useless.

The Instigator

My definition of an *instigator* is "a person who urges on, spurs on, or incites others to some action." Simply put, instigators always have some stuff going. An instigator should not be in your inner circle, but kept only as an associate. An instigator can't help him- or herself; this person has to gossip. Right now, I know you have someone in mind. I also know that you know better than to tell that person anything you don't want out in public.

I'm going to say something that you might not agree with: not all instigators are bad—especially when they're telling you something for your own good. So it's good to socialize with these people from time to time; they keep you updated about what's going on.

The power that instigators can give you is immeasurable. If you want to get anything out, just tell them, and if you want to know anything, just sit and talk with them awhile, and they'll tell you. But never under any circumstances let them pollute your mind with unhealthy information!

Every Time the Hater Sees My Friends, He or She Has Something to Say about Me

The stupidest thing a hater can do is talk about you to people who love you and have your back. Not only will the people who love you tell you what the hater said (which is what the hater wants them to do), but they are going to act as your personal spokespeople.

Beautiful! You couldn't ask for anything better. Your friends are your most powerful weapon; they can tell that person everything you'd want to say but can't say without acknowledging the hater's irritating attitude.

You have to keep in mind that the hater is not thinking logically; he or she doesn't care if these are your friends, and he or she probably didn't think they would go off on him or her. Just keep in mind that his or her friends, nine times out of ten, wouldn't do that for him or her. But the hater just hates you so much and wants you to know, because what he or she is doing (all the hating) doesn't seem to be affecting you, and that just kills the hater.

Remember, *you have the power*. Ignore negative people at all costs, because most likely, the people they're talking to don't matter anyway. Remember, birds of a feather flock together. So don't sweat the little stuff, because if they trash-talk you to someone who knows you, the person who knows your character won't accept the information anyway.

Conclusion

A person does not have the power to make you feel or do anything you don't want to feel or do *unless* you give the person that power. Remember to avoid all of that foolishness; stay out of these kinds of people's circle. If you are in the circle, believe me, they will fight to keep you there, even lie about you to keep you in your place. Ever heard the expression "crabs in a bucket"?

I was sitting under a tree a couple of years ago, drinking with some of my so-called friends. One of our partners pulled up; he had just gotten another job that paid pretty well, and he was talking about some of the things he was going to do with the extra money—all positive. He made a comment about not sitting under the tree and drinking anymore. That's when one of the guys said, "Aw, hell, you give a man a lil money, and he think he's too much. Man, you aren't no more important than anyone under this tree."

On that day, I started noticing all the little remarks that were made from then on. Why do you think that statement was made? Maybe the guy was scared of being left behind, or maybe he was just trying to keep the other guy in line and not let him think he was better than anyone else. Ask yourself: Was he right for making that statement? Remember, too, that the guy he was talking about was right there under the tree with him.

CHAPTER 3

CAN MY KINFOLK BE HATING?

What? You mean to tell me my family could be hating on me? Not my family! Besides, all my family members love me, right?

Wrong!

One of the most common things to expect is family members saying you think you're better than everybody else, just because you are starting to make some positive changes. But don't let that get you down, because as long as you stay real with your family, the real ones will keep it real with you. This is especially true of the elderly, because they will see right off what you're doing: changing for the best.

The ones you grew up with will probably have a problem with you, but just stay real with them. If they can't accept your positive change, then, in the words of Bernie Mac, "F them," and I really mean that. Don't lose focus for anybody, not even your family, especially if what you're doing will benefit the family as a whole and lay a foundation for the next generation.

You may say, *"But, EJ, you haven't told me how I will know if my family members are hating on me or not!"*

You'll know, because you will see it and feel it. If for some reason you can't see it or feel it, here are some hints. Take them to heart.

Do I have your attention? Just checking.

The first thing you will notice is that when you come around, your family members will make little smart remarks about what it is you're doing—meaning your positive change.

They also will give you the cold shoulder, but remember: just be yourself and keep it real. Most of them will come around, but for those who don't, just remember what Bernie said. Keep in mind that family is probably going to be your worst critic, so if you can make it through them, you'll be all right.

You might think your family is unique when it comes to this type of behavior, hating on each other, but you're not alone. Even if your family is rich, there are haters among them, and rich people are just as bad as the less fortunate when it comes to hating, but I will get to that point later.

You might say, "My family is poor . . . I mean 'ghetto fabulous,'" and I still say that is no excuse. It doesn't matter how rich or poor your family members are; hating is hating.

Rich Family Members Who Hate

The first thing to understand about rich family members who hate on you is that they are very jealous people. They see your advancements inside the family as a threat to their happiness—especially if it gains you respect in the family—because right now, *they're* the big deal.

These people will most likely never change, because they are self-centered and have to have all the attention all the time. Most family members who have money and hate will do everything in their power to keep you down or at least under them. Keep in mind that only haters do this, because most rich family members welcome other family members with open arms if they've made a positive change. Believe me, you would probably get more resistance from the less fortunate than from rich people. (I call this the "crap in the bucket mentality.")

The reason rich people may give you a lot of love when you change for the better is because they know you're going to see how much hell they've been catching, so welcome to the club! I'm not going to spend much time talking about family, because you don't get to pick them, but your friends' hell? That's your problem.

Ghetto-Fabulous Family Members Who Hate

These family members who are hating on you will most likely never change, because they already know you. If you change anything about yourself to appease them, they will only see you as being a fake. Keep in mind, it's not *you* they're hating on; it's your positive change, because in their eyes, you're acting like you're "all that." They are your family; they know all the things you did before your so-called positive change, and they don't mind reminding you either.

Remember that these people grew up with you. To them, you are Peewee, Bebe, Pookie, Heavy, Tiny, Rudy, or Rabbit, and now you want to act like you've got it together. How dare you! Family will always be family, and it's those little things they do that make them unique, whether it's making you laugh, smile, think, worry, fuss, get mad, or whatever; that's your kinfolk!

Conclusion

This is your family. Who knows your family better than you? Like I said early on: we can't pick our family, so whoever notices the positive change you have made, run with those family members. I don't know any family on earth—rich or poor—who get along all the time or with all of their family members, so welcome to the party, and good luck at the next family reunion. My advice on this topic is to love these family members the same but handle them differently, because most of them just can't believe it's you doing what you're doing.

"Nothing is as embarrassing as watching someone do something that you said could not be done."–Sam Ewing

---

CHAPTER 4

HATERS ON THE JOB

Yes, haters are even at your job, but I know for a fact you know exactly who they are. Believe it or not, your boss knows too, and you must use this to your advantage, to run haters off if necessary. Just in case you don't know who they are, let me give you some pointers on what to look for.

When you are running late, look for the person who makes the announcement that you are not where you're supposed to be. This person will ask people if they've seen you. He or she doesn't want anything; he or she just wants to let certain people know you're not there.

Another thing haters do is ask you questions that they already know the answer to in front of your boss. "Hey, EJ, how is that project coming along you've been working on since last week?" Of course they know exactly where you stand and know that you are running behind schedule, but they want your boss to know.

You might say, "EJ, you were late, and yes, you are running behind schedule." What I'll say to you is that *you* are that person I'm talking about: the hater. *You* don't take into consideration why I was late, and *you* don't take into consideration why I'm behind schedule. Maybe the reason people do these things is because they are always messing up and want to have some company (after all, misery loves company), or they have it in for you. Maybe they are just assholes, and they're just doing what assholes do.

But the hater is watching everything you do, and I mean *everything,* from what time you get in to what you are eating for lunch. You may ask, "How do I handle this person?" Rule number one: do your job, and do it well. Secondly, you have to fight back. This is your job; this is how you feed your family. So ignoring this person is the worst thing you can do. This person is not only attacking you but also your family, so whenever you get a chance to expose his or her faults and weaknesses, do it and this those not make you a hater besides you are protecting yourself.

You don't want to look like you have some petty competition going on, so use the brown-noser—the kiss-ass, the person on the job who tells the boss everything. You know who I'm talking about. Every workplace has one; hell, some places have two. Just let the brown-noser know, and he or she will do the rest. Make sure you tell him or her the little things you're doing that help the company—the things you don't get paid for and that may not even be part of your job. Believe me, it will get back to your boss.

Do not pity the hater or lose any sleep over this person, even if he or she loses his or her job. Remember, this was not just about you. When a person starts messing with your livelihood, you'd better fight back.

"When someone hits you, you hit them back, only you hit back twice as hard as they hit you."–Momma

---

You really shouldn't pay haters any mind, but when they cross the line and do things that affect your family, you have to take them out. The first rule of life is self-preservation, and family equals self.

If a hater is just hating on you but not jeopardizing your job and has no power to affect your job, then pay the person no mind; just don't put him or her in your inner circle or anywhere around you. Simply enjoy the look on the hater's face as you get promoted and begin to make more money and you're able to make key decisions, like hiring and *firing*.

If you find yourself in a position to fire that person, look for a replacement as soon as you can, and give the hater his or her pink slip. Trust me: you don't need someone around doing a particular job that might affect the good work and impressions you are trying to make for your boss. If that person gets a chance to mess you up, he or she will, and it will all be done out of hate. This is ridiculous, especially if you have not done anything to this person. Get rid of haters. A job is much easier when everyone is on the same page.

"The wise man must be wise before, not after, the event."–Epicharmus

---

What If It's My Boss Who's Hating?

There are two reasons I can see your boss hating on you. The first reason is if you are more established than he or she is. That's usually found in a boss who's younger than you are, but nevertheless, it's a problem. This problem can be fixed in most cases; you and the boss probably don't run in the same circles because of the age gap.

Let that person know that in a few years, if he or she keeps doing what he or she is doing, maybe the boss will even have more than what you have now. Be kind of a mentor to the youngster.

Another reason—and pray to God that this is not it—is competition for people you are both attracted to. If it is the reason, you are going to lose and lose badly. Leave the person your boss is after alone, or you will find yourself looking for another job—period.

Now, if for some strange reason that person your boss is after is your spouse, you have my permission to whip his or her ass.

Conclusion

Your job is one of the most important things in your life, so guard it well. My closing thought on this subject is this: if you tried to talk to your boss about the situation and he or she is still hating, I suggest you prepare yourself to find another job. If that person is a hater, there's nothing you can do to change the way he or she feels. There's not much you can do in a situation like this. Besides, he or she is the boss.

But there is one thing I recommend: consider starting your own business. Find out what you are good at and passionate about; then proceed with the necessities to succeed. That way, you won't have to worry about the foolishness of a hating boss.

CHAPTER 5
NOT MY SIBLINGS TOO!

I know what you're thinking: *Now that's a damn shame, for brothers and sisters to be hating on each other.* It's true, but sadly, it happens all the time. This problem usually stems back to early childhood. Maybe it started with the parents showing favoritism for one child over the other, or one felt the other was more attractive. Maybe one is better at sports than the other one. The reasons can vary, and it's really hard to tell.

When dealing with close family, by which I mean brothers and sisters, the way to look at these things is this: if you have nothing to do with the matter, *mind your damn business,* especially if you don't really know what's going on. This is a delicate issue.

If you know the family and you're not a moron and you have noticed the situation firsthand, speak to someone in the family, not in the streets. Notice I said *the family,* preferably an elderly person or a woman each one of them respects highly.

The reason I recommend an elderly person or a woman is because women have a natural, God-given instinct for seeing both sides of a problem and getting to the bottom of it. Now, in my opinion, if I had to give God a sex, I would say the Creator is a woman which I know is equally erroneous to saying the creator is a man. Don't like it? Prove me wrong. "But, EJ, the Bible says . . ."

Prove me wrong.

The good thing about the conflict is that it can be fixed, especially if the person who is doing the hating wants to fix it. Nine times out of ten, the hater just wants the other person to know what he or she felt at that time or is still feeling. If, for some reason, the person doing the hating doesn't want to talk about it and wants nothing to do with his or her sibling, there is nothing you can do about that. If the hater doesn't want to change his or her mind or at least talk, the same rules should apply. Love these haters the same; just work with them differently, but not for one second should you turn your back on them. Don't be their *fool*.

Man, I Think My Momma's Hating

What? Your momma is *not* hating on you. If anything, your momma knows you better than anybody on this planet, and she won't cut you slack when you're trying to get something over on her.

Even a momma who is not a good mother loves to brag about her children, especially if that child is doing well. I'm not even going to spend time on this subject. What I think you need to do is take a look in the mirror and re-evaluate yourself. I bet that within you lies the problem.

Man, I Think My Daddy's Hating

He might be. Besides, you never did get that paternity test. Men are better taking credit and acknowledging a child than a woman—once that child starts doing well and the success is widely known. Men love to brag about their kids, even if they had nothing to do with the success. But if a dad is hating, the same rules apply: love him the same; just work with him differently.

Conclusion

Siblings are going to fight; there is no doubt about that. But believe me, even though they may have had a big fight, the love is still there. If the hate is in someone's heart so deep that he or she refuses to even solve the issue, that's bad, and believe me, hate is just as strong as love, if not stronger.

For example, al-Qaeda and other radical groups hate the United States of America so much that they are willing to strap a bomb on their own kids. The way I see it, they hate the USA more than they love their kids, because I don't hate anyone enough to strap a bomb on my child; I don't care who said to do it. That is not common sense, and we know common sense is not always common.

"What luck for rulers that men do not think."—Adolf Hitler

CHAPTER 6

MAN, I THINK I'M THE HATER

The first step toward getting rid of a problem is admitting you have one. Let's not confuse hating with just not liking someone, because there is a difference. Let's say someone rubs you the wrong way; there's just something about this person that you don't like. It could be the way the person talks (crudely), the way he or she dresses (provocatively), or maybe the way he or she treats other people (disrespectfully). Those are not grounds to be called a hater.

Let's say this person has never done you any wrong. You were friends or at least associates. The person has now made a positive change or may have acquired something that you may have wanted or did not want; nonetheless, you are pissed off. My friend, if this is the case, then you are what some might call a hater.

Don't panic just yet, because just the fact that you acknowledge it proves there is hope for you. Let's check your symptoms. This might be a minor case of jealousy, which is treatable. Do you get irritated when that person comes around? Do you talk negatively about that person when he or she is not around? Do you do things intentionally to hurt that person, physically or mentally? If the answer to these questions is *no,* then you are not hating on this person—you may be jealous, but you are not hating now. If the answer is *yes,* then Houston, we've got a problem.

The Two Types of Haters

1. **The quiet hater.** This person is dangerous and very sneaky, the type who throws a rock and hides his or her hand.

2. **The loudmouth.** Loudmouths cannot help themselves; they have to show you they don't like you and let everyone else know they don't like you.

These two people are really one and the same; it's just that the quiet hater is a little harder to spot when you're not actively looking. The loudmouth is very easy to spot; he or she wants to be spotted.

If you find yourself in one of these two categories and really want to stop feeling like a hater, the only advice I have for you is to change your way of thinking, because behavior extends from thought. If you run around all day thinking, *I don't like this person,* then nine times out of ten, you are not going to like that person.

Let's say you cannot stop thinking about this person. Then my advice to you is to change your perspective about that person, because your perspective ultimately becomes your reality. If you can perceive that person in a different light, then whatever way you see that person in that new light will become your new reality of him or her.

You might still be saying, "Man, EJ, I just don't like that person." That's cool, as long as it's not because of a positive change that person has made or because of material things that person might have. If it is because of those things and you just can't help it, get yourself grounded in a good, faith-based church, because only the Lord can help you. The Lord still gives you a choice.

> *"Self-hate is a form of mental slavery that results in poverty, ignorance, and crime."—Susan L. Taylor*

Man, I Know I'm Hating

If this is you, all I have to tell you is, "Now listen closely."

That's all I have to say to you about your little hating situation. To anyone who may not understand what just happened, refer back to chapter 2. Go ahead and read the very first paragraph. I'll wait.

Now that we are back on the same page, let's keep it moving. Just remember: give haters no power. As for you, I doubt very much that you are a hater, for the simple fact that you are probably laughing at haters or yourself right now. One thing I have learned is that 90 percent of the time, haters do not laugh at themselves. It's too personal for them. Trust me, they see their faults as a handicap that you are trying to expose.

Rather than acknowledge their weakness and strengthen it, they hide it, so whenever the weakness is exposed, it cripples them. Family, you have to learn how to laugh at yourself, especially when a person is making fun of you and not doing it out of hate but out of good, clean fun and love. Just the fact that you even consider yourself a hater shows that you are concerned about your emotional state when it comes to feeling bad about something you know isn't right (like hating).

Haters don't have that problem, because their feelings are self-centered, meaning "it's my way or no way," and it doesn't bother them if you like it or not.

Conclusion

My friends, the fact that you are even worrying about being a hater is more than enough proof that you are not a zombie—I mean, a hater—so stop it. You have better things to do with your time than worry about if you are hating on a person, because I'm willing to bet that person is an asshole (pardon my French). Stay focused on you and yours, and help people when you can, and you will be all right. As for as the hating, leave that to the professional haters. They expect more bad out of life than good, and they expect to fail more often than they succeed, so let them get their shine on.

"No one can make you feel inferior without your own consent."—Eleanor Roosevelt

CHAPTER 7

DON'T EVEN KNOW ME AND HATE ME

This can't be happening. You mean to tell me this person doesn't even know me and is hating on me? What did I do to this person? The answer is *nothing*. Crazy, right? Let me explain.

In a situation where someone is hating on you and you don't even know the person, only two things could have happened. Either the person has been talking to one of your haters, or he or she just doesn't like your style. You say, "EJ, that makes no sense. I don't even know this person." My answer to that is never try to make sense out of nonsense; it will drive you crazy.

What you are trying to do is take something that is completely illogical and make it logical; it doesn't fit, and it's frustrating. Stop trying to figure these people out; you have to be crazy to even think about accepting their way of thinking. Let me explain the two reasons why haters do what they do.

If a hater has been talking to the person who hates you for no reason then, believe me, he or she doesn't like you. But cool off; that's only based on the hater, which can be corrected. First, if that person actually does spend time around you and is not a hater but had just gotten bad information about you, while you guys are socializing he or she will see the true you and change his or her mind about you. Once a person see you for who you are, that's when the magic starts, because now this person sees and knows how the hater manipulated perceptions of you shaped their views of you, and that is priceless.

Your haters don't like your style, you say, which is cool. Maybe you are too loud, or maybe you are too in-your-face; maybe you really think you are the deal, and you're not. Those are pretty good reasons not to like you, wouldn't you say? Sometimes people just see themselves in another person, and two demanding personalities just can't make it. (I call this "too-many-chief-and-not-enough-Indians-syndrome"; with this combination, nothing gets done.)

In this deal, you must be yourself; don't be what you are not. Never back down to someone who doesn't deserve it, but please know when you are out of your league. One of the greatest qualities of a leader is recognizing one who is greater. Remember that.

To put it simply, the person who doesn't like you for no reason other than what someone else told them is probably a bitter, small-minded, following chickenshit anyway. So don't lose any sleep over that, especially if he or she never tried to find out for him- or herself how you really are. Just stay grounded on what it is you're doing, because if you are not working with the Lord, then you are working against the Lord.

Haters Are Like the Flu—They're Contagious

If you ever take the time to notice, haters will always seek out other haters. Misery loves company. That's because they need supporters of their actions in order to feel like what they are doing to you is okay. That is the reason for the recruiting; the more, the merrier. If the hater gets enough people to think like he or she thinks, then these feelings are just. People have to be able to filter out nonsense and just know what kind of people are giving them information. Why someone would take something and just run with it is mind-boggling, but it happens every day.

If you don't want to get that sickening virus called HIV (hater in-voluntary), I suggest you equip yourself with the proper equipment: a level, strong mind and zero tolerance for bull. If people know you are like that, they won't even think about bringing mess to you. Why do haters try to get other people to hate you in the first place? The reason is simple. They need justification you are the problem and not them and besides, if you and that person ever met, and you both hit it off, then the hater has another enemy—at least that's the hater's perception I know it sounds crazy but look at the crazy people we are dealing with.

Learn how to eat the fish and spit out the bones.

If you don't want to catch the flu, then don't hang out with people who have it. Does that make sense?

This means you should have the willpower and insight to leave things and people alone who mean you no good. You simply have to walk away. If you can walk away from a thing or person, it has no power over you; you are the master, no matter how juicy the news is. The ability to present you with information and have you accept it as reality is too much power for a person to have over you. Think.

I Trust My Source

If the person who you are getting your information from is a stand-up person, and you respect his or her judgment, then there's no problem. Just know who you're talking to.

When a person tells you something about another person, there's a motive behind it, good or bad. Only your true friends' motives are usually always good. Just remember, we always get what we ultimately deserve, whether we like it or not. So if your friend is telling you something about another person, pray to God you haven't sowed a bad seed somewhere that's coming back to you.

No matter what haters do or say, if you are supposed to have something, whether it's good or bad, you will get it. Karma is a bitch.

Learn to trust your friends; they are your eyes and ears when you are not around, so when your friends stand up for you it's a beautiful thing. In the words of Ronald Reagan, "Trust but verify."

Conclusion

There are many reasons why people could be hating on you even if you don't know them, but who has time to figure these people out? Here are two of the main reasons why they do might hate on you, based on my research. Haters love company and will seek it out wherever it is. Stay focused on you and yours, because there's nothing you can do about what others are doing or saying. Hang around with like-minded people, preferably people who are smarter than you. That way, you'll learn something; remember, iron sharpens iron.

For the people you don't know who are hating on you, thank God you don't know them. Look at who they're socializing with—they're probably socializing with haters. I don't judge people based on their money or how many college degrees they have. I know people who have money coming out of their asses who are miserable as hell. I know people with more degrees than a thermometer who are dumb as hell. Don't get me wrong; I think money and education are very important. I rank them right up there next to breathing, so please don't get it twisted.

CHAPTER 8
MAN, NOT IN THE CHURCH!

You mean to tell me haters are in the church house too? The answer is yes.

"What can they possibly be hating on in the church?" you ask. Anything that makes them feel uncomfortable. It could be the way someone dresses, the way someone sings, the way someone tithes, the way someone doesn't tithe, or the way someone preaches.

The first thing you must understand is that the church house is a place to fellowship and worship your God but some people can make it one of the messiest places going, in my humble opinion. That's the place where most people young and old go to catch up on what's going on around the neighborhood, rather than what going on in their hearts and it's where most of the children learn how to talk about people.

Don't believe me? Notice your beloved church before and after services; check out all the meetings going on. I wonder what they're talking about.

"Damn you, EJ, not my church! Everybody in my church is a good, God-fearing Christian." Oh, I'm sorry. I wasn't talking about *your* church. I was talking about those *other* churches. Your church is cool.

She Didn't Have to Dress Like That

This applies mainly to women, because most men really don't care about how another man dresses for church. "Girllll, did you see that dress so-and-so had on? Now she knows she was wrong for that. I mean, you saw how high and tight it was . . ." That's the women's perspective. Now for the men: "Mannnn, did you see that dress so-and-so had on? Now she knows she was wrong for that. I mean, did you see how high and tight it was?" They said the same thing, but I assure you that these two conversations had completely different meanings.

Nine times out of ten, the dress probably wasn't that high and probably not that tight. You see, most men (not me) usually exaggerate things. Hell, some women can't look at a man without him thinking she wants him. Most women are just plain jealous of other very attractive women, especially when they know they are getting attention.

Women are constantly checking out other women's clothes. "Girl, that was a bad dress so-and-so had on." That's no problem as long as it's tasteful, but haters don't care how nice the dress was. To them, it was trashy.

Men, please remember this: if your girlfriend or wife asks you if you saw the dress that the woman was wearing, say, "Hell yeah," and make sure you say it was trashy too. You can act a fool and say, "Man, she was wearing that dress" if you want to. You'll mess around and can't go to that church anymore without arguing about what she had on this Sunday, because your girlfriend or wife is just going to automatically think you are looking—which you probably are.

Ladies, if you are not out of line with your clothing selection, don't sweat it. I'm sure that in your life, you are probably used to these problems with other women just hating on you because you're beautiful. To you I say, "Keep on doing you, girl." If you're out of line, I'll say this to you: "Ho, you need to put some clothes on. Where do you think you're going, to the club? You're going to the house of the Lord, and besides, there's children in here and also God-fearing Christians who don't play that—well, at least not at this church."

He or She Always Has to Sing

This is very funny to me, and by now, you should have noticed I have a great sense of humor.

Check this out: A person who can't sing but wants to sing is getting mad at another person who can sing and is singing crazy well. I told you these people are crazy. Now keep in mind it's not just about that person singing; it's mainly about the *attention* that good singer is receiving for their talent. You see, haters are bitter and mad about their lives and can't stand to see anyone—I mean *anyone*—getting positive feedback, which they feel they can't get. That just kills them.

Let's say you always sing in church, and everyone knows you can sing, but you have a bad morning and sound pretty bad. Guess who will be burning with excitement, going around telling everyone who will listen how terrible you sounded? If you can sing, and you know that person is hating on you for something as silly as that, every time you sing, and I mean *every time,* just look at the hater and smile and keep on blowing.

Because what can you do about it? By now, you'd better know the answer to that question.

Why Do They Put So Much in Church?

"He knows he didn't have to put that much money in church. They ain't doing nothing but showing off."

Boy, those haters are something else. Give too much and they talk about you; don't give enough and they talk about you. If you think that's bad, try not tithing at all. Now you are a lowdown, dirty MF.

Just because of comments like the one above— accusing the giver of "showing off"—and that way of thinking, God is never going to bless haters. It's solely on the condition of their way of thinking, which filters down to their hearts. That way of thinking just isn't right. If God blesses you with the ability to give in abundance, and you want to give, then give. You will be damned if you do and damned if you don't, and there is nothing you can do about it.

These are born-again Christians. I guess they were baptized in lemon juice, because some of them are bitter as hell. Seek prosperity, and you will attract prosperous people; that's the law of like attracts like.

"Anyone who comes in your life and cannot give you one of these things, money, support, or shelter, is not sent by God but by the devil, to stop your progress."–Bishop E. Bernard Jordan

---

I Hate the Way He or She Preaches

"I can't stand when Reverend So-and-So preaches. He or she just talks people's business."

Ever heard that one before? Now for the real reason: the Word is probably convicting them, and they just can't handle it.

Have you ever been in church, and the pastor started preaching on a subject, and you'd swear before God that he or she was talking directly to you? That's called your conscience, and in good people, when they do wrong, it usually bothers them. But for haters, not only doesn't it bother them, but they get mad at anyone who tries to awaken that conscience.

Sounds like the devil to me. Preachers have the ability to disturb that spirit in people, and haters don't like that. This is why when pastors talk about positive things, most haters remain quiet, but when the pastor gets to talking about negative things like the love of money or pride, haters start whooping and hollering. That's their connection.

To the pastors in church who are preaching from the heart and not aiming the message at a certain person, I say let the Word of God convict these haters Keep on preaching. But for the ones who bring what people tell them in private, and it ends up at the pulpit, remember: God doesn't sleep.

Conclusion

You would think that the church house would be exempt from this nonsense, but you have to understand that the church is a building that's filled with regular people who are not always nice. I did not go as hard as I wanted to go on this subject. Keep in mind that the truth hurts, and this is just volume one.

Even in the church, every savior needs a devil or demon to battle. That is one reason they're in church in the first place. So keep a sharp eye out in church, because when someone has done something wrong, the first place he or she usually runs to beside momma house is the house of the Lord. That's also another reason haters go to church: to be able to come back and say, "Girllll, you will never guess who came to church today!"

You can have people sitting beside you in church, and you don't know why they are there; they can be there for forgiveness or just to soothe their own guilty conscience. Please don't take offense to this, because remember, these types of people don't go to your church, right? Thank God for that, now if you are in church for all the right reasons may God continue to bless you with a clean open mind and a pure heart Amen.

SUMMARY

What have we learned? Let's think. One thing is that haters would rather tell you, "I'm sorry that happened to you," than, "I'm glad that happened for you." We have also learned that haters have some great qualities: they are consistent and persistent. These are very good traits to have; the problem is, haters just use them for the wrong reasons.

Haters also always worry about how people view them, meaning they always think people are talking bad about them. They always blame other people for their own shortcomings and do absolutely nothing to correct their faults or at least improve them. They see the world as a bad, cruel place, and if you have "made it" (based on their definition of making it), to them you have done something wrong to get there. They think you shouldn't be congratulated but condemned. In their world, they decide whether or not you are too good to socialize with. Misery loves company, and the more people at the party, the better it is. Can you even imagine a party with no one but haters there? One of the quickest ways to spot a hater is by his or her body language. Another way is by his or her negative remarks, the envy he or she shows when you come around, or if your name is even mentioned. Haters get irate when speaking with you, and you actually feel the vibes that they are transmitting.

Note: I said it earlier, and I'll say it again: please do not socialize with these people. Keep them as far away from you as possible. They are nothing but snakes, biding their time.

What can we do about haters? The answer is *absolutely nothing,* so don't try. Haters have been here since the dawn of time. They're not going anywhere, so equip yourself with the knowledge to spot them and deal with them. Remember, give them no power; completely ignore them when possible. Keep them out of your circle of associates, and keep notice if they are physically trying to harm you. Never under any circumstances take pity on them. Haters should be completely alienated or at least contained. Make no mistake about it: this is a war, and I'm sad to say that right now, they are winning.

Think about every time people talked you out of doing something you felt very passionate about. If you listened to them and didn't do it, they won. Remember every time people made you give up on a project you were doing, just because it was a slow process and the results were not manifesting right away. If you listened and gave up, they won. Every time you allowed them to control the way you think by not even being able to talk about your dreams and goals, they won then too. Because you knew they would only laugh at you and call you crazy for thinking like that, so you suppressed the dream and let them win.

"Our doubts are traitors, and make us lose the good we oft might win, by fearing to attempt."—William Shakespeare

---

There is one thing that must be present for a hater to be happy: conflict. When you are depressed and going through troubles, haters are celebrating. They need you to be miserable for them to be happy. I can only think of one other entity that has that trait, and that is the devil.

Keep in mind that most of your haters were once your friends or at least your associates, so just remember it's not you that they are hating. It sounds crazy, but it's true; they really just want their friend back. If that means stopping you from moving forward because that is the process that's making them look bad, then stopping you is what they have to do. Whenever you start doing something positive, the naysayers will always surface.

Naysayers are mirror images of haters; they talk about all of the problems but don't have any solutions. I really believe they are just telling you the things they can't do or the things they tried to do and failed, which left them mentally poor. The poorest person in the room is not always the person without a nickel in his or her pocket, but the person without a goal or dream in his or her head. If your past looks brighter than your future, then you're in big trouble. You see, winners refuse to be defined by the days behind them but by the days in front of them, because they know that is where their legacy lies.

You have to climb over your history to get to your destiny, and haters are put there by the devil to anchor you down if you let them. So don't worry yourself with haters, because if you do, you will only make yourself mad. You are doing it to yourself, and that's self-inflicted frustration, which you don't need.

If you have any inspirations or goals, go for them, and don't pay the haters around you any mind. Most of them will spend forty years building someone else's dream and won't spend one day on their empire. Family, choices have to be made. We all came into this world naked, scared, and ignorant, but we all learn as we go, and things get better as we get better.

Some people will argue you to death and say that we all are in the same boat. This is exactly the reason why everyone should be trying to get out of the boat. If you stay in the boat, all you will ever see is the disciples, but if you get out, then you can see Jesus. Now you'll need some faith just to attempt to step out of the boat. All of your senses, family, and friends will be telling you not to get out, screaming that you can't do it, that you are going to fail.

Vision comes before provision; you first have to see yourself doing what it is you want to do in your mind, and then move toward that direction. That old cliché is right: if you can see it, you can achieve it. So stop getting mad at these haters and giving them a piece of your mind, because that is one of the reasons some of you don't have much left—you gave half of it away.

Haters only exist because we acknowledge them. Whatever doesn't get your attention really doesn't exist to you. When talking to people, remember that small people talk about people, and big people talk about ideas, so keep haters out of your thoughts and your conversations. Some people just mean you no good, especially when they are purposely trying to convey their shortcomings and bad life experiences to you, for the purpose of holding you down. Life lessons are learned as we go, and there is no class you can take to learn how to lie or do wrong. For some people, it just comes to them naturally. They are born haters.

I wonder if that's what God meant in Jeremiah 1:5 NLT when the Creator said, "I knew you before I formed you in your mother's womb." Talk to your kids about this early; let them know that there are some bad people in this world whose job is to hinder. The devil does not have a special age when he starts attacking your children, so arm them with the right equipment, so they will know how to sidestep these evil people at an early age.

Are haters necessary? I would like to think that they are, because they help push us further in life. Haters are nothing but batteries that keep us charged when moving forward toward our goals and dreams. Believe it or not, if you study and apply the teachings in this book, you will be able to use that negative energy of a hater and transform it into positive energy for you to use. Now you have just tapped into an unlimited energy source for your goals and dreams. Stay focused, and if you can, try to pick up one hater every month; if you do, that means you are making serious progress in your life. Keep your head up and move forward, because now you know how to spot and deal with haters.

Thanks to all you haters in the world, because without you, this book could have not been possible. Also I would like to thank all the people who regardless of the problems they have had; kept moving forward toward their goals and dreams you guys inspired me. I would also like to give a very special thanks to all the pastors out there who teach people *how* to think and not *what* to think may God forever bless you. See you on the battlefields.

THE END

Well, not really.

ABOUT THE AUTHOR

E. J. Tyler served four years in the US Army and has owned a business for the past six years. He is a father to six girls. He and his wife, Latricia, have been married for seventeen years and live in Louisiana.

NOTES

NOTES

NOTES

NOTES

NOTES

NOTES

NOTES

NOTES

NOTES

NOTES

NOTES

NOTES

NOTES

NOTES

NOTES

NOTES

NOTES

NOTES

NOTES

NOTES

NOTES

NOTES

NOTES

NOTES

NOTES

Made in the USA
Columbia, SC
26 December 2024